When Waiting Hurts

Learning How To Trust God's Process & Timing

Rev. Dr. L. Renee Gibson

Acknowledgements

I would like to first and foremost thank my Lord and Savior Jesus Christ for ALL that He's done for me, and for my being able to put these words to paper. It is a humbling and awesome experience. I want to acknowledge my family and friends for their consistent love and support. A special thank you to those who gave this project a "first read" during the editing process. I also want to thank those of you who have chosen to read this book, and I pray that it is a blessing to you.

Table of Contents

Introduction
"Waiting Sucks!"

Let's have a conversation about waiting. I'll begin, waiting sucks! You may be surprised by my opening statement, but if this book stands a possible chance of helping anyone, anywhere, honesty is important from the very start. That being said, I go back to my original statement…waiting sucks! It's tedious, it's boring, and we have to do it far more than we'd like. We wait in traffic, we wait in line at the bank, and we wait in line at the grocery store (usually behind someone with a cart that runneth over while we stand there with two measly items). We wait for the guys at the auto shop to finish with the car; we wait for our turn in the hair stylists' or barber's chair. We wait for vacation, we wait for payday (talk about waiting that sucks!). We wait, we wait, and we wait.

We also wait on God. We wait on God to get us out of those painful situations that it seems like we've been dealing with forever. We wait on Him to fix broken relationships, we wait on Him to repair torn marriages, and we wait on Him to make wayward children become the little angels they once were (you remember, back when they were about two minutes old). We wait on God to end our unemployment or heal our bodies. We wait on him to unlock the doors that will enable our most cherished dreams to come true. We even wait on God to help those we love with their situations. We wait, we wait, and we wait.

We start out waiting so patiently too, don't we? We pray and we quote every Scripture we know on waiting. Some of my favorites include Lamentations 3:25, "The Lord is good to those who wait for him, to the soul who seeks him," Micah 7:7, "But as for me, I will look to the Lord; I will wait for the God of my salvation; my God will hear me," and James 5:7-8, "Be patient, therefore, brothers, until the coming of the Lord. See how the farmer waits for the precious fruit of the earth, being patient about it, until it receives the early and the late rains. You also, be patient. Establish your hearts, for the coming of the Lord is at hand." And of course, there are two "classic" verses of Scripture related to waiting that I dare not skip. There's Psalm 27:14, "Wait on the Lord and be of good courage; wait I say on the Lord," and perhaps the most iconic Bible verse there is on waiting (at least in my experience), Isaiah 40:31, "But they who wait on the Lord shall renew their strength; they shall mount up on wings like eagles; they shall run and not be weary; they shall walk and not faint."

We wait so much that we even have songs about waiting, from traditional to contemporary. Juanita Bynum has one that was once pretty popular called, "I Don't Mind Waiting." In fact, that was pretty much the whole song, "I don't mind waiting. I don't mind waiting. I don't mind waiting on the Lord." I remember a church choir that used to turn church out with a song based on Isaiah 40:31, "I'm gonna wait on Jesus, gonna stand right here, I shall not move. I'm gonna wait on Jesus, I know my blessing is coming real soon. If you wait upon the Lord Jesus, he shall renew, renew your strength." They had an anointed choir director who knew how to let the Lord lead her through a song, and I'm telling you, by the time the choir got to the vamp at the end and the sopranos, altos, and tenors started singing, "He shall renew your strength" over and over...the church would catch fire!

But what do you do when you've been waiting so long that instead of quoting Psalm 27:14 you feel like quoting Habakkuk 1:2, "O Lord, how long shall I cry, and thou wilt not hear? Even cry out unto thee of violence and thou wilt not save?" or Psalm 6:3, "My soul is in deep anguish. How long, Lord, how long?" What do you do when instead of singing, "I Don't Mind Waiting," you really feel like belting out, "Pass me not, O Gentle Savior. Hear my humble cry. While on others thou art calling, do not pass me by!" What do you do when waiting doesn't just suck, it actually **HURTS**?

If you were drawn to the title of this book, if you picked it up and began to flip through it, then it's my belief that you're waiting on God for something: A new job? A better car? A spouse? A better relationship with your children? A closer walk with God? Deliverance from illness? Whatever it is, maybe you've been waiting on it for a while. Maybe you've been waiting on it so long that the waiting has begun to feel like torture. You've prayed every prayer you know how to pray; perhaps you've even fasted and prayed. You've been trying to be patient and wait on God, and you know that He is well able, but so far…nothing. Or perhaps in an even more painful fashion, there have been flashes of light which indicated that dawn was just about to break through and then wham! The darkness of waiting settled in again. If this sounds like you, or maybe someone you care about, then journey with me through the pages of this book. We're going to spend some time together talking about when waiting hurts and journey towards hope. It is my prayer that you will leave this book feeling at least a little bit better than before you came.

Before we get started, I want you to write what you're waiting for on the lines below:

1. ______________________________
2. ______________________________
3. ______________________________
4. ______________________________

Now, I'd like for you to pray the following prayer:

Dear God, I have been waiting on the issues that I wrote above, and the waiting has become difficult. I ask that you lead and guide me through this book and through this period of waiting in my life trusting you for victory in your time.
In Jesus' name I pray, Amen.

AUTHOR'S NOTE

There are several Scripture references that make up the framework of this book. An overview and explanation of these verses can be found in the appendix. All Scriptures are from the New International Version of the Holy Bible.

Chapter 1
"Deal with Reality"
Scripture Reference: Jeremiah 29:4-11

As a child I loved reading, and fables and fairy tales were some of my favorite reading material. One of my favorite fables was, "The Emperor's New Clothes." I don't know if people read fables as much as they used to, so let me give you the gist of the story. There's this emperor in a make-believe land who absolutely loves clothes; so much so that his reputation for fashion is known far and wide. One day two swindlers come to town and offer to make the king a suit out of this fabulous, magical cloth. What makes the cloth so special is the fact that it can only be seen by smart people who are worthy of their jobs. The king pays for the cloth and sets the swindlers up in a special sewing room. He sends different advisers in from time to time to see how his suit is coming. Now no one he sends in can see a thing, but they all come back and tell him how beautiful and how fabulous the suit is. The king decides that a suit SO grand should be displayed during a big parade. The day finally comes when the suit is finished, and the king gets ready for his parade. He goes in to see the swindlers who hold up his suit. He doesn't see anything, but when the swindlers say, "Isn't it grand your majesty?" and "Aren't the colors magnificent?" the king replies, "Oh yes!" The king doesn't feel anything as the swindlers pretend to put the suit on him, but he swears that the suit feels splendid and heads out for the parade. Everybody in the crowd oohs and aahs about this amazing suit made out of this cloth that only intelligent people can see, until finally a small child blows the whole thing up with the truth by declaring, "But he doesn't have anything on!"

That's kind of what Jeremiah does for the children of Israel in Jeremiah Chapter 29. Israel was God's chosen people, but they had a bad habit of disobeying God. They got themselves caught up in this vicious cycle of disobedience, get punished by God, repent, God would lift the punishment, and the people would obey…until the next time. After several cycles of this God told them (I'm paraphrasing), "I'm not going to keep talking to you, and evidently the current punishments aren't working. Just keep it up, and the punishments you got before are going to seem like nothing compared to what's coming. Just keep on!" The people kept on and God allowed Babylon to take them captive. He told them that they were going to be in captivity for 70 years. Now even though God has a reputation for doing just what He says He's going to do, the people convinced themselves that God wouldn't really leave them in a foreign land for 70 years. They even got some false prophets to "go look at the cloth" and agree with them. The false prophets even got as far as telling them that they didn't even need to worry about unpacking in Babylon because they wouldn't be there long!

Enter the Prophet Jeremiah with a dose of reality. God used Jeremiah to tell the people "Don't listen to those false prophets and those dreams that they are having. Don't listen to the dreams they are encouraging you to have. I didn't send them, and they don't speak for me! You're going to be there 70 years just like I said!"

So, what does all of this have to do with waiting that hurts? Sometimes the reason that we have to wait so long that it hurts is because we haven't dealt with the reality of our situation. We strut around like we're wearing a tailor-made suit and get other people to agree with us about how good it looks when in reality we're wearing nothing at all! We walk around pretending that life is all sunshine and rainbows when in actuality not only is the storm raging; there's a flood on the horizon! Now, let me pause here to make a disclaimer: I am not saying that when you're dealing with painful situations that you have to walk around sad and gloomy so that the whole world knows that you're hurting. Neither am I saying that you have to let everyone in the world in on your private business (even though **EVERYBODY** needs **SOMEBODY** that they can talk to when the going gets rough). What I am saying, however, is this: you do yourself a great disservice when you walk around denying the reality of your situation. If it looks like a duck, waddles like a duck, and quacks like a duck, then you need to stop telling yourself that it's a chicken and admit that it's a duck!

I'm going to let you in on a little secret…sometimes we have to wait in our current situations (even if the waiting hurts) until we deal with the reality of the situation and how we got there. Okay, let's pause for another disclaimer. There are some painful situations that we find ourselves in that we have absolutely no control over. We live in a fallen world and, as a result, sometimes bad things happen (even to good people), and we have to wait for things to improve (maybe not exactly a comforting thought, but remember this chapter is about reality). And yes, sometimes the waiting hurts. **HOWEVER**, there are other times when we end up in bad situations and we know exactly how we got there, but we won't admit it. Sometimes it's in those situations where we have to wait, and wait, and wait. We get tired, we get frustrated, and sometimes we say, "Lord, you said weeping may endure for a night, but joy comes in the morning! Where is morning?" I've got to pause her to say that sometimes we can't get to morning until we deal with why it's nighttime.

Let me try to make this a little plainer. Let's say you've been out of work for a while. You've been filling out applications, you've used your networking resources, you've mailed out resumes, and yet…nothing. Now let me ask a few uncomfortable questions. What kind of report can your last employer honestly give about you? What was your attendance like on your last job? Did you show up on time? Did you meet all of your requested deadlines whenever possible? Did you approach your job with an attitude of gratitude, or did you complain about it every chance you got to anyone who would listen?

Okay, let's try this scenario. You just can't seem to get your finances headed in the right direction. No matter how hard you try, you always seem to have more month than money! You've stretched your paycheck so far that it's just about to snap in two, and you still can't make it stretch far enough to make ends meet. Question time again! Have you taken the time to examine your spending to make sure that you're not buying things that you don't really need? Have you made a budget so that you can prioritize your spending? Most importantly, have you taken your tithes and offerings to the house of God? (I know tithing can be a sticky subject for some folks but **BELIEVE** me when I say obedience is better than sacrifice!)

When waiting hurts, you've got to deal with reality. You've got to ask yourself the hard questions about where you are and how you got there. You've got to spend some time talking and listening to God about your situation, because even if the bad situation happened due to circumstances beyond your control the One who's in control may still have something for you to learn from it. Get yourself some strong, trustworthy, Spirit-led counsel who can help you sort through the reality of your situation by telling you what you need to hear even if it's not what you want to hear. Take a good, honest look at the situation and yourself. Dealing with waiting that hurts requires dealing with reality.

Reflection

As you think about the situations that you're waiting on are there any actions you've taken that may be contributing to the wait? Is there anything that you feel God may be trying to teach you in your current situation? Write your answers below:

____

____

____

____

Prayer

Dear God, please give me a mind, heart, and spirit to look at the reality of my current situation. Help me to honestly examine my part in how I got here. Show me what it is that you would have me to learn about You and myself in this situation. Lead me to wise counsel and order my steps as I wait. In Jesus Name, I pray, Amen.

Chapter 2
"Hands Off, God!"
Scripture Reference: Proverbs 3:5-6

All is such a tiny word; just three little letters. When taken at face value it almost seems insignificant when you consider the fact that the English language has such magnificent words as honorificabilitudinitatibus (the state of being able to achieve honors), floccinaucinihilipilfication (the estimation of something as valueless), and then there's my personal favorite, hippopotomonstroesquipedalian (an adjective pertaining to extremely long words!). I may as well confess that I have no clue as to how to pronounce any of the examples that I just gave, but my point is this; "all" looks kind of puny in comparison, doesn't it? Yet, as tiny as a-l-l is, it packs a powerful punch. All means, "The whole, entire, total amount, quantity, or extent of." It is used to emphasize the greatest possible amount of a quantity. In simpler terms, there's nothing outside of all!

The definition of the word all is especially important to our reference text for this chapter, Proverbs 3:5-6. "Trust in the Lord with all thine heart and lean not to thine own understanding. In all thy ways acknowledge Him and He shall direct thy paths." Let's take a closer look at the first part of the text and what it means to us when waiting hurts.

"Trust in the Lord with all thy heart." I want to take a minute to rewrite that verse using the definition of the word all as well as the definition of the word trust. When you rewrite the verse using those two definitions you get, "Have assured reliance on the character, ability, strength, and truth of God with the whole, entire, total amount, or quantity of your heart." Read that again slowly for me please. Finished? Now let me say it in plain terms, "Trust **God** with your whole heart because of who He is!"

Why is that so important? It's important to trust God with all of your heart because, "Out of the heart comes the issues of life." (Proverbs 4:23) Every dream that you have comes from your heart. Every desire that you have comes from your heart. Each and every action that you take in your life ultimately comes from your heart. I became an educator because a love of children resides in my heart. In my heart of hearts, I believe that children are one of God's most precious gifts to the world, and are deserving of all the love, guidance, and nurturing that we can give them. My love of children runs so deeply that I literally can't pass a baby without smiling and, most of the time, they smile back. They often reach for me to pick them up even if I don't know them. My family calls me "The Baby Whisperer," but I believe that children just know instinctively that they are dear to my heart. From the love of children rooted in my heart came a career in education and the role of biological or adopted auntie to over 20 children-and counting!

Who we are, how we act, the decisions we make-all of these are influenced by what resides in our hearts. Therefore, it's important for us to trust God with our hearts which allows Him to shape our desires, decisions, and actions.

Let's connect this to when waiting hurts. Chapter one of this book talked about dealing with reality, and the reality is that sometimes we have to wait in our situations because we're not trusting the Lord with ALL our hearts. We have certain parts of our heart that we've declared off limits to God. We tell ourselves that those areas are our responsibility. Sometimes it's because we've been disappointed in that area. Sometimes it's because we're frustrated with the wait. Sometimes it's because we're afraid to give God complete control. Whatever the reason, we refuse to give God of all of our heart. The problem with that is that the very part of our heart that we're withholding may be the very part that God needs us to trust Him with the most before He can give us what it is we've been waiting on. It's that part of our heart that he needs to work on in order for us to be ready to receive and maintain that precious blessing that we've been waiting for.

Let me lay out some examples. You've asked the Lord to give you a better job, but you don't trust Him to show you the best way to prepare for it. You've been praying for your relationship with your spouse to get better, but you don't trust God to lead you to figuring out and fixing what went wrong. You've been pleading with God to heal your broken heart, and you've been pleading for a long time. You've cried and prayed, fasted and prayed, worshiped and prayed, and your heart is still broken. You're waiting for restoration and healing, and the waiting hurts! But there's something important that I need you to understand. Sometimes we're waiting on God to put our broken hearts back together, but in reality He's waiting on US to give Him all of the pieces!

Sometimes when waiting hurts we have to ask ourselves some hard-hitting questions. We have to honestly ask ourselves if we are truly trusting God with all our heart, or if there are some parts where we've told God, "Hands off!" If there are pieces of our heart that we are withholding from God, then we need to prayerfully ask

Him to help us relinquish them to Him. You can't expect to make a good cake if you hold back some of the ingredients: you can't finish a jigsaw puzzle without all the pieces, and sometimes you can't get to your blessing until you trust God with **ALL** of your heart. Is there a part of your heart that you're holding back from God? If so, write it in the blank space in the prayer below; then sincerely pray the prayer as often as you need to until you've given God control of your whole heart.

PRAYER

Dear God, I humbly acknowledge that you are sovereign
Lord of all. I acknowledge you as Lord
of my life through my faith in Jesus Christ. Father, I admit that
*I've withheld the*____________________________________
area of my heart from you.
I repent and ask you to take control of my whole heart.
Help me to have assured reliance on your character, ability,
strength, and truth.
In Jesus name I pray, amen.

Chapter 3
"God What Are You Doing Here?"
Scripture Reference: Proverbs 3:5-6

This chapter will be a short one since it relies a lot on the information about the word "all" presented in Chapter Two. Our focus is the beginning part of Proverbs 3:6, "In all thy ways acknowledge Him." I promise that this book will **NOT** be heavy on the vocabulary lessons, but I need to go over the definition of the word acknowledge. Acknowledge means, "to recognize the rights, authority, or status of." It also means, "to express gratitude or obligation for." Now let's do what we did in Chapter 2 and rewrite the Bible verse using the definitions of "all" and "acknowledge": "In your whole, entire, total way of life recognize the rights, authority, and status of God with gratitude and obligation."

In other words, you have to recognize God's authority over every part of your life. It is imperative that we recognize that God is the Creator, and we are His creation. This means that we belong totally to Him as His children based on our faith in His Son Jesus Christ. He is the ultimate parent. Let's think about that parent thing for a minute. For most of us as children, there was no part of our lives that was off limits to our parents; our business was their business. They imparted knowledge into us, taught us right from wrong, and raised us to exhibit certain behaviors everywhere we went. It's the same way with God. God gives us knowledge about who He is and how He requires us to behave as His children; and He expects both to influence every aspect of our lives.

This means that we can't decide to let God be in control of our lives and our behavior on Sundays from roughly 8:00 to 1:00 (depending on your church's hours), then decide that Sunday afternoon through Saturday night is our shift. We can't allow Him to be in charge of our lives at home but decide that we don't need His guidance at work. We can't give God control of our children but declare our marriages off limits. All means all!

Let's get back to the painful waiting. Sometimes when the waiting hurts, we have to ask ourselves if there are parts of our lives that we are leaving God out of. We need to ask ourselves if we're pleading with Him to fix one part of our lives while leaving Him out of the rest. These questions are important because if we want God to do great things in our lives then we have to give Him control of our entire lives. As I said in Chapter 2 asking God to fix part of our lives without giving him control of the rest is like asking someone to do a jigsaw puzzle without all of the pieces; no matter how hard they try the puzzle can't be completed! And here's another important tidbit of information: God isn't going to snatch the puzzle pieces. He wants us to voluntarily trust Him and give Him control of our lives willingly. He wants us to submit our entire lives to Him because we trust that He knows what's best for us and will take care of us.

Sometimes waiting hurts because we're not acknowledging God in every aspect of our lives. We can't ask God to bless us in one area of our lives while expecting Him to stay out of the rest. All means all!

REFLECTION

Are there areas of your life where you're leaving God out (work, marriage, etc.)? Write them on the lines below:

1. ______________________________
2. ______________________________
3. ______________________________
4. ______________________________

PRAYER

Dear God,

I come to you in humble submission as your child through Jesus Christ. I acknowledge that there are areas of my life that I often leave you out of. I repent Father, and I ask you to help me to truly and fully acknowledge your authority over every area of my life with trust and gratitude to you. In Jesus' name I pray, amen.

Chapter 4
"Don't Stop in the Swamps of Sadness!"
Scripture Reference: Jeremiah 29:4-11

In preparing the second message of the series of sermons that ultimately led to the writing of this book, "What Do You Do Until?," the Lord brought back to my remembrance a movie that I saw a few times as a child. The movie was called, "The Neverending Story," and it was about a little boy who was on a quest to save a mythical land called Fantasia. The boy traveled on his beloved horse, Artax. During the course of their adventure they have to cross a place called the Swamp of Sadness.

They had been warned by an ancient creature in the story to be careful to keep moving while crossing the swamp; they are warned not to let the sadness take over or they will sink and die. As they are crossing the swamp, the little boy's horse gets sadder and slower. Artax eventually stops and the little boy begins to beg him to start walking again. He pleads with Artax to keep moving, reminding him that if he doesn't move he'll die. The horse doesn't listen, and the next scene shows the little boy sitting at the edge of the swamp crying with the end of the reigns in his hands, and his beloved horse, Artax, buried under the mud.

When waiting hurts, it's so tempting to stop moving and just sit still in any one of the depressing swamps that extended waiting can create. There's the swamp of our circumstances; our unemployment, our sickness, our broken marriage, our lingering singleness, our strained finances, our wayward children, our unsatisfying or stressful jobs, or (insert your situation in the blank). There's the swamp of self-pity as we ask the Lord, "Why me?" There's the swamp of frustration as we watch doors open for others while the one we're knocking on with all our might seems firmly shut. There's the swamp of despair as days of waiting turn into weeks, months, years, and maybe even decades with relief seemingly nowhere in sight. Extended waiting can create a lot of swamps around us, and if we're not careful, we will fall into them, stop moving, and drown.

So how do we keep moving through the various sad swamps that waiting can create? We do what Jeremiah told the children of Israel to do. Remember in the first chapter of this book I told you that Jeremiah shattered the people's false hopes that their time in Babylon would be less than the 70 years that the Lord had promised. Jeremiah let them know in no uncertain terms that they would be there for the full span of their punishment. But he didn't tell them to sit still and cry about it. He urged them to build houses and live them. He urged them plant gardens and eat what they planted. He urged them to get married and have children and not only that, he told them to marry those children off so that they would have grandbabies. Jeremiah even told them to work for the peace and prosperity of Babylon so that it would be a better place for them to live since they had to be there anyway. In other words, Jeremiah urged the people to be faithful and fruitful right where they were!

What do you do until you get a new job or a better job? What do you do until your boss stops making the office feel like a living hell? What do you do until your marriage gets better? What do you do until your finances improve and there's finally more money than month? What do you do until your body is healed? What do you do until **THAT** situation gets better; you know… the one that nobody knows about except you and God? What do you do until…?

What you do is make sure that you don't stop moving in the swamps of sadness. Let me pause to make another disclaimer: I am not telling you to be content or pretend to be happy about a bad situation. Even though we are filled with God's Holy Spirit we are still human beings, which means that when the waiting hurts we feel sad, we feel frustrated, we feel discouraged…we hurt. I understand that and I wouldn't be callous enough to tell you not to feel what you feel. However, what I am telling you is this-don't let your feelings keep you from doing the best you can, while you can. What you do until is make sure that you remain fruitful and faithful right where you are even though the waiting hurts.

Let's talk for a minute about what remaining faithful and fruitful looks like in practical terms. It looks like going to work on time and doing the work you've been hired to do even if you can't stand the job, your boss, your co-workers, or all of the above. It looks like praying for your mate (and **NOT** that they get zapped by lighting) and treating them as well as you can for as long as you safely can. It looks like following the doctor's orders (all of them) and taking the medicine, he gave you. It looks like continuing to pray, worship, serve, and obey the Lord our God showing that even though you're still waiting, you trust Him enough to keep walking by faith through the swamps of sadness until you reach the other side! Don't stop in the Swamps of Sadness!

REFLECTION

How can you recognize when you've stopped in the "Swamps of Sadness?"

1. ______________________________

2. ______________________________

Which swamps do so seem to stop in most often ("Why Me", "Despair", "Anger", "What If", "If Only")?

1. ______________________________

2. ______________________________

What can you use as your catalyst to get moving again? (Ex: Pray, phone a friend, go for a walk, listen to your favorite song, etc.)

1. ______________________________

2. ______________________________

PRAYER

Dear God, as I think about my situation, I hurt, and sometimes that hurt keeps me from being as productive as I can be. Father God, I ask you humbly and sincerely in the name of Jesus to help me not let frustration and despair overwhelm me. Help me to continue to trust you and help me to be faithful and fruitful in my current situation until better comes. In Jesus name I pray, amen.

Chapter 5
"Get Over Your Own Understanding!"
Scripture Reference: Proverbs 3:5-6

We as human beings really think that we're smart. Why shouldn't we? We know more now than we've ever known before, and we have instant access to anything that we don't know thanks to Google, Siri, and Alexa. There's also a self-help book for just about every subject you can think of. Just out of curiosity, I checked out the Barnes and Nobles online self-help section and they offered me 213,411 titles. No wonder we think we're so smart!

In fact, we believe that we're so smart that we can figure out God's plan for our lives and do a better job of carrying it out than God can, in spite of the fact that in Proverbs 3:5-6 the Word of God tells us not to lean on our own understanding and to allow God to direct our paths. We believe it in spite of the fact that the same Word of God tells us in Isaiah 55:8-9, "My thoughts are not your thoughts, nor are my ways your ways; For as the heavens are higher than the earth; so are my ways higher than your ways and my thoughts higher than your thoughts." Now, just as a frame of reference, let's think about the fact that the sun is an average of 93,000,000 miles away from the Earth which means that if you could drive there doing oh, let's say about 80 miles an hour, it would take you 1,162,500 hours or 132 years to drive there! This is how far God's thoughts are from ours, and yet we still try to outthink God!

We really try to outthink God when we're waiting for something and the waiting hurts. When the waiting hurts we tend to begin to lean on our own understanding. We figure that God's working too slowly. We believe that we know the plan just as well or better than God and we begin to come up with our own ways to move things along. Sadly, this usually just makes us have to wait longer, and usually causes us more pain on top of the already painful waiting.

Let's talk for a few minutes about a couple of familiar biblical characters, Abraham and Sarah. God promised them a son even though they were already well past childbearing years. In fact, God promised Abraham that he was going to have too many descendants to count. Time goes by, however, and there's no baby, which does not bode well as a good start for endless descendants. Sarah leans to her own understanding and decides to help God out by urging Abraham to have a baby with her maid, Hagar. Abraham agrees and Hagar gets pregnant. The situation soon becomes complicated because Hagar begins to hold it over Sarah's head that she's managed to give Abraham what Sarah couldn't---a baby. God let them know in no uncertain terms that this was **NOT** what He had in mind; He said that Abraham and Sarah would have a baby and that's what He meant! Sarah took matters into her own hands because the waiting hurt and her actions resulted in an ugly family conflict that's still affecting the world to this day!

When the waiting hurts, we have to be careful to get over our own understanding. Our understanding is finite and is often based on what our situation looks like, seems like, or feels like. Our understanding is incomplete because we don't know all that God knows and we don't see all that God sees. Our understanding is limited by the fact that we can only see yesterday and today while God sees yesterday, today, tomorrow, and forever more. Our understanding is flawed, to say the least, and we need to get off of it!

It is imperative that we trust God and our relationship with Him even when waiting hurts. We have to allow Him to lead and guide us through this topsy-turvy, crazy, and sometimes frustrating thing called life. When we're trying to move from one stage or event in our lives to the next, we've got to trust God's plan and timing even when it seems to be taking forever and the waiting hurts. We've got to trust that God knows what He's doing even when we can't see the light at the end of the tunnel.

The Word of God says that we walk by faith and not by sight (II Corinthians 5:7). That means that sometimes you may not be able to see your desired outcome on the path God's called you take. But, if that's the path He directed you to, keep walking. You may not understand the action that He's urging you to take in the midst of your waiting, but He doesn't need you to understand, He just needs you to obey! Okay, now it's disclaimer time again. I am not advocating rash, hasty, or foolish actions. You need to use common sense, logic, and sound decision-making skills in life. If you've been fired from your job, it's probably not a good idea to keep showing up every morning like you still work there expecting God to miraculously give you your job back. However, if you're looking for a job and God persistently puts it on your heart to reach out to a friend that you haven't spoken with in years, you might need to get over your own understanding, ignore the fact that it doesn't seem to make sense, and make the call! It might not seem to make sense to you to go back to school right now, but if God keeps placing it on your heart, if you can't seem to get it out of your mind, if the concept seems to be everywhere that you turn, then you might need to get over your own understanding and sign up for at least one class. When the waiting hurts we have to walk by faith using the spirit of discernment, and contrary to popular belief, discernment doesn't always mean understanding!

REFLECTION

Are there any actions you've felt God leading you to take in this season of waiting? List them below and then put an asterisk (*) by any that don't seem quite logical to you.

PRAYER

Father God, I know that you know what's best for me. Please give me a strong spirit of discernment in this season of waiting. Help me to trust and obey you even when I don't understand. In Jesus name I pray, amen.

Chapter 6
"Sometimes It's Necessary"
Scripture Reference: Romans 8:26-32

I'm going to make a statement right now that I pray doesn't make you close this book and toss it across the room (and if you do, it's okay, but after you calm down, please pick it back up and finish it.) Okay, here goes: sometimes the waiting needs to hurt. Sometimes we need to feel the sting of working, watching, and waiting, with morning seeming no closer. Sometimes we need to get our fingers slammed in the closing door and then stand there nursing our bruised fingers while hoping, praying, and yes, waiting for the door to open again. Sometimes the painful wait is necessary.

I'm sure at least one person reading this book is now wondering why I would make such a statement. Why should we have to wait for something so long that the longing in our hearts actually seems physically painful? How in the world could I have the audacity to say we need that kind of torture in our lives? I can say it because the Word says it. Romans 8:28, which is one of my favorite verses of Scripture, reads, "And we know that all things work together for the good to them that love God, to them who are called according to his purpose." That particular verse of scripture is a popular one that's often used for encouragement among Christians, but I want you to go back and read it again for me. Notice that while it says that all things will work for our good, it does not say that all things will be good.

Early on in this book we talked about the definition of the word "all", and the fact that there's nothing outside of "all". That means that when it comes to life we need to realize that there will be good **AND** bad. We're going to have to deal with some days when we feel like we're on top of the world and some days when we feel like the world is on top of us! This includes dry seasons of waiting until the waiting hurts.

Here's another not-so-pleasant, but hopefully helpful statement: Sometimes we are not ready for what we're waiting on and we don't know it, but the God who knows all and sees all does! He knows that we aren't physically, emotionally, financially, or, maybe most importantly spiritually ready for that thing we're longing for with all of our hearts and so He holds on to it. He holds on to it because He knows that if He gave it to us right now we wouldn't be able to handle it and it may very well end up destroying us. So He makes us wait, even though the waiting hurts.

God has good things in store for His children who walk in faith and obedience to Him, but sometimes we have to take the long route to get to them. You see, sometimes it's the pain and struggle of waiting that helps us to make the best of our blessings when we finally get them. One of my favorite examples of this is the story of

Joseph which begins in the 37th chapter of Genesis and continues to chapter 50. God had big plans for Joseph's life, and Joseph got a glimpse of those plans through his dreams. The problem was that Joseph's father and especially his older brothers didn't appreciate Joseph's dreams when he shared them because they showed Joseph, the younger son, in a position of authority over all of them. Joseph's brothers were so angry that they threw him into a pit with the intention of letting him die, but they settled for selling him into slavery. Joseph's life took him from visions of greatness at home to a pit, to being a slave, to being falsely accused of attempted rape and thrown in prison, to being left waiting in prison by someone HE helped encourage in their season of waiting! It was only after all of this that Joseph ended up being second in command to Pharaoh and was able to save his family from a devastating famine. The story ended on a high note, but the waiting had to hurt! I mean, can you imagine sitting in jail for a crime that you didn't commit, looking at your present circumstances while thinking about the bright future you thought you saw for yourself? Yet, if Joseph hadn't gone through each and every one of those painful experiences he wouldn't have gotten to the palace that made his dream a reality! And who knows, maybe Joseph needed the time and the experiences to be mature enough to handle the authority he ultimately ended up with.

Sometimes the waiting needs to hurt. There are times when we simply aren't ready for the blessings we've asked God for and…sometimes it takes some rough experiences to get us ready. Sometimes we have to go through the pit to get to the palace. Let me use a concrete example. Sometimes it might take a painful divorce or failed relationship and a long period of singleness for us to be ready for that "Til death do us part," marriage. Sometimes God may have to take us through a long period of unemployment and financial struggle so that when we finally get a new, higher-paying job, we're able to make the most of the money. Sometimes we have to stand in the rain so that we can truly appreciate the sunshine. Sometimes even though the waiting hurts, it's necessary.

Reflection

How have some of the not-so-pleasant experiences in your past made you better?

What's one way that the "extra" time in this season of waiting can help you be ready for your blessing?

PRAYER

Dear God,

The waiting hurts, but I know that you have better in store for me. Please help me to learn whatever it is that you need me to learn in this season of waiting. Please help me to view this time of waiting as a time of preparation, trusting you that all things will work for my good because I love you. In Jesus name I pray, amen.

Moving Time

We've talked a lot in the last six chapters about the pain of waiting. We've talked about dealing with the reality of our situations. We've talked about yielding all of our heart to God and giving God control of every aspect of our lives. We've talked about what we can do to avoid drowning in the swamps of sadness during the wait and how we've got to get over our own understanding. We've even had the uncomfortable conversation about the fact that sometimes the painful wait is necessary. **NOW**, it's time to talk about moving towards hope.

Chapter 7
"Use Your Resources"
Scripture Reference:
Romans 8:26; Ephesians 6

It can be difficult to wait while God is working on our behalf; especially if the waiting has begun to hurt. Sometimes we get impatient and try to help God along in the process. Sometimes we decide that it will hurt less to just give up. Sometimes we even get angry and rebel against God; we stop praying, giving, worshipping, you name it! Sometimes we struggle in the waiting!

One of the reasons that we struggle so hard when the waiting hurts is that we don't use all of our resources.

When we're in what I call the "workroom of life," waiting on God to open the door to our blessings, we often act as if we're on our own, and that can't be further from the truth. God has blessed us with resources in the workroom of life and, if we use them, they might just help the waiting hurt a little bit less.

The first tool that we have is our faith. "Now faith is the substance of things hoped for and the evidence of things not seen," (Hebrews 11:1). Faith in Jesus Christ is what opens the door to a relationship with the Father. Faith is what allows us to please God. Faith is what opens our hearts to dreams and possibilities. Faith is what enables us to start working towards making those dreams reality, and faith is what helps us keep going when waiting for the materialization of those dreams hurts.

Another powerful resource we have at our disposal is prayer. I'm going to talk more about prayer in the next chapter, so all I'm going to say right here is that it is one of THE most important resources that we as Christians have at our disposal, and we need to be sure to use it daily.

An additional resource that we often underutilize is the Word of God. The Bible is full of stories about people who had to wait, and we can probably see ourselves in some of them if we look. Some waited for a loving spouse. Some waited for a baby. Some waited for healing for their loved ones or for themselves. Some waited for deliverance from oppression. People waited in the Old Testament and the New Testament, and their stories can help us to remember that we're not alone. The Bible also gives us practical instructions for daily living and can help us to see when we might be contributing to the waiting. For example, James 1:6-8 tells us that when we ask God for something we have to ask in faith and not doubt that He can deliver. James says that we can't expect anything from God if we're wavering back and forth about whether or not God can come through. We've got to be like the three Hebrew boys who when facing certain death, declared, "God may not deliver us from this situation, but we know that He can!"

There's another powerful, powerful resource that we don't use enough when waiting hurts. In the 14th chapter of John Jesus promised, "I will ask the Father and He will give you another Comforter that He may abide with you forever." Jesus promised a Comforter that would teach us and help us to remember His teachings. That Comforter is the Holy Spirit. God sent His Holy Spirit to dwell inside each of us from the moment that we confess His Son Jesus Christ. He sent the Holy Spirit to teach us and guide us. He sent Him to comfort us in our weakest and most painful moments including in the workroom of life when the waiting hurts.

The Holy Spirit is a powerful resource if we take the time to recognize Him and allow Him to work in our lives. The Holy Spirit is that "something" on the inside of us that speaks to us when we're confused and helps us to discern our next move. It's the "something" that leads us to that person who gives us just the right advice or encouragement at just the right time. The Holy Spirit is that "something" that helps us keep going when we want to quit. The word of God tells us that the Holy Spirit is even that "something" that makes intercession for us with God when we can't pray or don't know what to pray for! Talk about a powerful resource!

God doesn't leave us to fight our battles alone. He loves us too much for that. He equips us for our journey through life, including those painful waiting periods in the workroom of life. The problem is that we don't always take advantage of all of the equipment. Faith, prayer, the Word of God, and reliance on His Holy Spirit can help us when the waiting hurts…if we let them.

Reflection

Of the tools listed above, which do you use most often in this season of waiting? Which ones do you think you could use more effectively? Write at least one goal for more effectively using the tools of faith, prayer, the Word of God, and/or the Holy Spirit.

____

____

____

____

____

Prayer

Father God, I thank you for giving me resources to help me in this season of waiting.

Please help me to use every resource that you've given me.

In Jesus name I pray, amen.

Chapter 8
"The Power of Prayer"
Scripture References:
Ephesians 6:18, Romans 8:26

I said in the previous chapter that prayer is one of the most important resources that a Christian has, and it is. The Word of God has several verses of Scripture that encourage prayer. "If my people, who are called by my name will humble themselves and pray, and turn from their wicked ways, then I will hear from heaven, and I will forgive their sin and heal the land," (II Chronicles 7:14). "The Lord is near to all who call on Him, to all who call on Him in truth," (Psalm 145:18). "Pray always with all prayer and supplication in the Spirit…" (Ephesians 6:18.) If you need more compelling evidence about the importance of prayer, let's take a look at Jesus. Jesus prayed. Jesus prayed a lot. He prayed before performing miracles, He prayed for other people, He prayed for His enemies, and He prayed when facing the darkest moments of His human life. Jesus Christ, Son of the Living God, took time to pray. Prayer is important.

Every child of God needs a healthy prayer life and, truthfully, you need to develop it before waiting hurts. I often say in sermons and teachings that rough times just aren't the best time to develop a rapport with Jesus. To me that's kind of like calling up a distant relative that you really only know through family stories and trusting them to support you through a crisis. You think that they might based on the stories that you've heard, but you haven't spent enough time with them to be sure. But fear not. Even if you feel like your prayer life isn't all that it could be, or if you feel like it's been slipping, you can get back on track.

First of all, make prayer a priority. In the book, The Battle Plan for Prayer: From Basic Training to Targeted

Strategies, the authors suggest having a scheduled time and place for prayer. I agree with this suggestion because we are creatures of habit and talking to God at the same time each day may ensure that we talk to Him daily. I make it a point to set my alarm each morning to allow at least 30 minutes where I can commune with God through prayer before I get up to start my day. I also make sure that I talk to Him before I lay down at night. Those are my scheduled times to talk to Him, but sometimes I also talk to Him throughout the day as well. I like talking with God and more importantly, I need to talk to Him. It's just too hard when I don't. Do you have a regular time when you have a little talk with Jesus? If not, over the next few days I want you to be conscious of your time. Look for a time period in your day that seems to be consistently slow enough and peaceful enough for you to spend some time with God; then commit to spending that time with Him every day. Oh, and by the way, there is no magic time frame. You may spend five minutes in prayer or you might spend an hour or more; the time frame isn't what matters. What matters is loving God enough to dedicate some part of your day-everyday to conversation with Him.

Another key to a healthy prayer life is remembering to pray beyond our wants and needs. I know that you picked up this book because you're waiting on something, and you've got something specific to talk with God about, but that can't be the only thing that you talk about! How would you feel if the only thing you heard from your spouse, kids, or friends was, "I want," "I want," "I want?" (Okay, some of you may actually be dealing with that right now, which means you should **REALLY** get the point I'm trying to make here.) God wants us to bring Him our fears, hurts, sorrows, desires, and wants. He truly does, but He also sometimes wants us to acknowledge the things He's already done in our lives. Sometimes He wants us to be honest with Him about our sins and say that we're sorry. Sometimes He wants us to pray for other people so that we can remember that our lots could always be worse, and sometimes He wants us to just acknowledge that He is truly an awesome God! A healthy prayer life is a well-rounded one.

A healthy prayer life also means realizing an often-overlooked fact about prayer. Prayer is not just a one-way street where we do all the talking and the conversation is over when we say, "Amen." Prayer is talking and listening to God. Sometimes we're stuck in waiting that hurts because we're asking God to unlock the door so loudly that we can't hear Him telling us where He put the key! Sometimes we need to just be still after praying and ask God to speak to us. How does He speak? It depends on the person and the situation. Sometimes it's an unexpected phone call after you've prayed for guidance. Sometimes it's a song, Bible verse, or passage of Scripture that seems to be directly related to what you just prayed about. Sometimes it's a feeling so strong that it almost seems audible. Sometimes it is just a settling in your spirit and heart that everything will be okay even if it doesn't look like it yet. God speaks if we're willing to listen. You just have to make sure that you talk to Him enough to discern His voice and His leading.

The most important key to a healthy prayer life is one that we talked about in the last chapter, faith. If you're going to talk to God about your problems, then you're going to have to have faith that He's listening. Why take your deepest cares and concerns to someone if you're not sure that they're going to listen or care? You're going to have to trust that God loves you and that He wants to hear from you. You've got to believe that the Holy Spirit will speak for you when you don't know what to say or maybe you hurt too much to be able to say what you need to say at the moment. Above all, you've got to believe that when you go to God that He is able.

When the waiting hurts, pray. If the waiting still hurts, pray some more. If the waiting has caused you to lose faith, pray and ask God for more faith. If the waiting hurts so much that you can't pray at all about the situation anymore, then ask God to lead you to a strong, Spirit-filled prayer partner who will pray for you and/or with you until you can pray for yourself (I had to do this myself when one of the deepest desires of my heart seemed to be so far out of reach that giving up was easier than believing). No matter how long you've been waiting, and no matter how much the waiting hurts . . . pray.

Reflection

What's your scheduled prayer time with God? How often does this time get interrupted? What can you do to make sure that regular prayer time with God happens for you?

____

____

____

____

____

____

Prayer

Dear God, I thank you for the privilege of prayer. I ask that you help me to make time with you a priority. Give me a spirit of faith, wisdom, and discernment. Help me to rely on your Holy Spirit and trust you to not only hear me, but also speak to me in a manner that I can understand. In Jesus name I pray, amen.

Chapter 9
"Keep Watching for Morning"
Scripture Reference: Psalm 130:5-6

Most of us are familiar with the Bible verse in Psalms 30:5, "Weeping may endure for a night, but joy cometh in the morning." It's a comforting verse, it really is, but I'm reminded of a quote from one of my favorite books by Stephen King, The Green Mile. The Green Mile is the name given to the long hallway condemned prisoners walked down on death row during the 1930's in the fictional town of Cold Mountain. One of the main characters in the book, which is told through flashbacks from a nursing home, is a death row officer named Paul who is cursed with extraordinarily long life because he executed an innocent man who could perform healing miracles. The former guard is 104 years old, and he confides in a friend that he already longs for death though he knows that he still has many, many years in front of him. He says that night is the worst time for him as he remembers all of the family and friends he's seen die before him due to his advanced age. He goes on to say that everyone has to walk their own green mile in life, "...but sometimes, oh God, the green mile seems so long." Sometimes when the waiting hurts and we think about Psalms 30:5 we might feel like Mister Paul, "Lord I know that you said joy comes in the morning, but oh God the night seems so long."

You pray and you watch for morning. You fast and you watch for morning. You worship and serve God with your whole heart and watch for morning. You move as He directs you by faith and watch for morning. You watch and wait; and it seems like morning is no closer. The horizon is still dark; in fact there's not even a glimmer of light showing. It's still so dark and it's been dark for so long that a question starts to form in your mind. Is morning really coming? As you continue to wait, that question begins to come to your mind more and more often and the question seems to make the waiting hurt even more. Sometimes it begins to hurt so much that you start to wonder if it would hurt less to just let go and give up. Give up on getting a new job. Give up on getting married. Give up on saving your marriage. Give up on having a baby. Give up on your finances improving. Give up on your health improving. Surely, giving up and grieving a final time for the lost desire or lost dream would hurt less than the waiting.

Maybe you're in that moment right now. If you are, it's okay. I've been there more times than I want to admit. But, even if you've got your towel in your hand with your arm drawn back to throw it in, I need you to hold on to the towel for at least one more moment and believe me, this moment is critical. I need you to stop in this moment and read the words of Psalm 130:5-6 from The Message Bible translation, "I pray to God-my life a prayer-and wait for what he'll say and do. My life's on the line before God, my Lord, waiting and watching till morning, waiting and watching till morning."

I know that you're tired. I know that you're frustrated. I know that the waiting has become excruciating. But before you give up, I need you to remember that your very life is a prayer on the line before God, and He will not fail you. You've got to keep watching for morning!

Early on in this book I talked about facing reality, and the reality is that there are times when we need to put a period on some situations and close the book (please don't close this one yet!). There are some requests that we make to God that He doesn't grant because He knows that what we've asked for isn't what's best for us. Sometimes the answer is no and, as painful as it might be, we need to hear it, receive it, and move forward. But…

Be careful that you don't put a period where God wants a comma! Don't give up and close the book because you're tired of waiting on the next line of the story. Pray about it and listen for God to speak to your heart. If you trust God, really trust Him and your relationship with Him through His Son Jesus Christ, He will let you know when to let go and when to **KEEP WATCHING FOR MORNING!**

I'm reminded of the Biblical story of Hannah. Hannah's husband had two wives. The other wife had children, but Hannah didn't, and the other wife didn't let her forget it. She taunted Hannah cruelly and constantly because Hannah had no children. Year after year Hannah prayed and cried, yet she remained childless and tormented. The hurt became so great that Hannah didn't even want to eat. Hannah's husband loved her dearly and said to her, "Please stop crying. Please eat. Am I not worth more to you than ten sons?" Hannah stopped crying and ate to please her husband, but she didn't stop praying! She went to the temple alone and poured out her heart to God with such silent fervor and passion that the priest thought that she was drunk. Hannah assured the priest that she wasn't drunk--just aching with the pain of waiting. The priest prayed for Hannah and before the end of the year Hannah- childless, tormented Hannah-Hannah who'd prayed for years seemingly to no avail, embraced a baby boy named Samuel which means, "I asked God for Him." She kept watching for morning!

If your dream is still in your heart and God hasn't given you peace with letting go, **don't give up!** Keep watching for morning. People may call you foolish. Well-meaning friends might encourage you to move on to something else. You may even feel slightly crazy for continuing to wait, but if deep down inside you feel like God is telling you to trust Him and keep waiting, then no matter how long it's been or how badly it hurts, **keep watching for morning!**

REFLECTION

What would it take for you to totally and completely give up on what you're waiting for? Why did you choose that as your signal? Pray about it for at least one week (talking and praying with a strong prayer partner might be good during this time) then reevaluate whether or not you truly believe that's the signal you need.

I feel like I need to let go of waiting

for________________________ if and when

____

____

____

After a minimum of one week of prayer…

How do you feel now about what you wrote above?

____

____

____

PRAYER

Dear God,

I have been waiting on resolution for my situation, and the waiting hurts. Sometimes I'm tempted to just give up. Please speak to my heart and help me to trust you and your will for my life. Help me to know if ***YOU*** *want me to keep watching for morning and give me the strength to keep doing so knowing that in your time, morning will come. In Jesus name I pray, amen.*

Chapter 10
"When Morning Comes"
Scripture References:
II Kings 5:5-11 & Luke 17:11-19

This book has talked a lot about what to do when waiting hurts, and I pray that something you've read thus far has been a blessing to you. I pray that you've read something that will help you move towards hope while you wait.

But there's something else that I need to talk with you about. What do you do when the waiting is over? What do you do when you finally get the new job, or you get married, or there's actually a little surplus in the bank every month? What do you do when morning comes?

I wanted to include this chapter in the book because I'm convinced that, sometimes when morning comes after a long night, we end up right back at midnight because we don't know how to handle morning. We're like those individuals you see in documentaries who won the lottery, or a big game show and ended up bankrupt because they didn't know how to handle the money. We don't always know what to do when morning comes.

So how do you handle morning? One of the most important things that you need to do when morning comes is make sure that you don't miss daybreak! In II Kings 5 there's the story of a man named Naaman. Naaman is an important man with a lot going for him, but he has a disease called leprosy. Leprosy was a painful skin condition that also carried a tremendous amount of social stigma. Naaman is advised to go see the prophet Elisha about his condition and he does. Now when Naaman and his entourage get to Elisha's house, Elisha sends word to Naaman to go wash seven times in the Jordan River.

Naaman goes away furious! You see, he thought that he could have taken a dip in one of the rivers back home if that's all it took to make him well. He figured that the prophet would at least come out, touch him, and pray over him, calling on his God to heal Him. Naaman was not pleased! Luckily, before he could get in his chariot and leave in a huff, some of the people with him urged him to follow Elisha's directions. They said to him, "If he'd told you to do something complicated and difficult to get rid of this disease, you would; so why not just go wash in the water?" Naaman follows the directions and he's completely cured.

Naaman got cured, but think about it. He almost missed out on his cure because it didn't come the way he thought it should! He almost missed daybreak! If we're not careful, we'll do the same thing. We've been praying and waiting, and praying and waiting, and then we miss daybreak because it doesn't come the way we expected it to.

Let me share something important with you about God. God is going to do what's best for us according to His will and for His glory. That means that sometimes even when He gives us the desires of our hearts, He may not give them to us the way that we expect. Sometimes that dream job may open up, and it's ours for the taking, but we may have to move away from the only town we've ever known. Sometimes the perfect man or woman comes into our lives, but they seem to be the exact opposite of the kind of person we saw ourselves with. Sometimes the baby we've longed for comes from an unexpected source. When that happens, we have to be careful not to miss, ignore, or toss out our blessings because they didn't come in the package we expected. We've got to be careful not to miss daybreak.

Another important thing that we need to do when morning comes is make sure that we don't forget to give God thanks for our deliverance. Even though Naaman threw a temper tantrum when he didn't like the solution, once he was healed he went back to the prophet to offer a gift of thanks and acknowledged the God of Israel as the only true God. He had enough sense to say thank you, and so should we! God wants and expects us to. If you read the story of the ten lepers in Luke 17, you find that of the ten who were healed from their leprosy, only one came back to Jesus to say thank you. Jesus doesn't miss the ingratitude either. "Were not ten of you cleansed? Where are the other nine?" Sometimes we get so caught up in celebrating morning that we forget the morning-maker, and that's not good. God is loving, gracious, generous, and merciful, but He does not want to be taken for granted. When morning comes, be careful to take the time to give God praise for it.

There's one more thing that I need you to be sure to do when morning comes. I need you to make sure that you stay close to Jesus. You see, a sad, but true fact is that the better things are, the further away from Jesus we sometimes get. When the waiting hurts, when it's still dark outside, we talk to Jesus a lot. We pray morning, noon, and night. We read the Scriptures searching for answers. We meditate on the Word and ask God to speak to us, lead us, guide us, and strengthen us as we wait for morning. But when morning comes… sometimes when morning comes, we don't talk to Jesus as much as we used to. We don't read about Him as much as we used to. We don't visit the House of God like we did when it was midnight. I call it a situational relationship.

Let me say something about this situational relationship. Be careful. Be very careful because a situational relationship with the Lord is not a healthy one. You've got to make sure that your relationship with God is a priority during the bad days and the good days. You're going to need His help to be a good steward over your blessings. You're going to need His guidance to maintain what He's given you. You're going to need Him just as much in the sunshine as you did in the rain. You've got to stay close to Jesus.

It's a beautiful thing when morning comes. Before I retired my job had a long commute and I was often on the road in the wee hours of the morning when it was still dark outside. It was amazing to watch the blackness disappear as I rode along, and it was even more amazing to watch the sky become lighter and lighter until it was ablaze with the full glow of morning. It's beautiful when daybreak comes in our lives too, especially when it's been dark for so, so long. We need to make sure that we appreciate the beauty of morning and handle it correctly.

Reflection

As you think about the situation that you're waiting on, what do you think will help you make the most of morning?

____

____

____

____

____

Prayer

Dear God,

As I continue to watch and wait in faith, I ask that you prepare me for when morning comes. Help me to be ready for my morning however you choose to send it. Help me to have a heart that remembers to thank you for my morning, and a heart that remembers to put you first at all times. In Jesus name I pray, amen.

Conclusion
"Waiting Still Sucks!"

Well, we've made it to the end of the book. Now let me go ahead and say what you might be thinking. Waiting still sucks! I get it. In this instant, microwave, ask Siri and Alexa, get-it-now society that we live in, waiting is not popular. It's especially hard when we're waiting on some of the deepest desires of our hearts, and we've been waiting for a long time. Waiting sucks!

Even if that's still your sentiment on waiting, it's my sincere prayer that this book has and will make waiting suck just a little bit less. I hope that something that was written in here will make the waiting process a little less painful. I encourage you to go back through this book if you get a chance and highlight anything that was particularly helpful. I urge you to read and reread the Scriptures in this book, as well as any other Scriptures that speak to your heart as you wait. Continue to pray the prayers found in this book-in addition to your own. And above all else, keep praying, keep believing, keep working, keep watching for morning; and be ready when morning comes.

PRAYER

Now unto Him that is able to do exceeding, abundantly above all that we ask or think, according to the power that worketh in us; Unto Him be glory in the church by Christ Jesus throughout all ages, world without end. Amen.

(Ephesians 3:20-21)

Appendix
Scripture References

There are references to several verses of Scripture throughout this book. Some of them are explained in the chapters they're found in, but there are three passages that I want to provide clarity for separately for anyone who might need it.

The first passage is Proverbs 3:5-6, "Trust in the Lord with all thine heart and lean not to thine own understanding. In all thy ways acknowledge Him, and He shall direct thy paths." The book of Proverbs, written primarily by King Solomon, is considered a book of wisdom. It's called by many Biblical scholars a practical guide for daily living. According to inspirational writer John C. Maxwell, "It's a book of simple yet profound wisdom designed to improve the way we think and therefore act." I need to pause here to make sure that we understand something about wisdom. Wisdom is more than intellectual knowledge. We can have knowledge of a vast variety of things; however, wisdom is the ability to apply that knowledge. For example, I have knowledge of healthy eating and exercise habits, but I'm still working on wisdom in those areas (sigh).

The second passage of Scripture that we need to take a look at is a bit longer and it comes from the book of Jeremiah. Jeremiah ministered to God's chosen people during the last forty years of the nation's history. He had the uncomfortable task of confronting the people about their constant disobedience to God and the devastating punishment on the horizon for them. In the short passage of Scripture we'll be focusing on for this book, Jeremiah has to dash false hopes, confirm harsh conditions, challenge self-pity, and offer hope; no easy feat. Jeremiah 29:4-11 says, "Thus saith the Lord of hosts, the God of Israel, unto all that are carried away captives, whom I have caused to be carried away from Jerusalem unto Babylon; build ye houses and dwell in them; and plant gardens and eat the fruit of them; take ye wives and beget sons and daughters; and take wives for your sons, and give your daughters to husbands, that they may bear sons and daughters; that ye may be increased there and not diminished. And seek the peace of the city whither I have caused you to be carried away captives, and pray unto the Lord for it: for in the peace thereof shall ye have peace. For thus saith the Lord of hosts, the God of Israel; Let not your prophets and your diviners that be in the midst of you deceive you, neither hearken to your dreams which ye cause to be dreamed. For they prophesy falsely unto you in my name: I have not sent them, saith the Lord. For thus saith the Lord, that after seventy years be accomplished at Babylon I will visit you and perform my good word toward you, in causing you to return to this place. For I know the thoughts that I think toward you, saith the Lord, thoughts of peace and not of evil, to give you an expected end." Jeremiah was telling them that even though God was going to bring them out of Babylon, they were going be there every day of the 70 years that the Lord told them they would spend in captivity. Sounds like some waiting that hurts, doesn't it?

The third passage of Scripture that's an important part of this book comes from Psalm 130. The book of Psalms is considered one of the poetry books of the Bible. If you've ever had an opportunity to read through the book of Psalms you know that there seems to be a Psalm for just about every range of human experience and emotion in this thing called life-from fear and discouragement to triumph and praise. The two verses focused on in this book center on hope. Psalm 130:5-6 says, "I wait for the Lord, my soul doth wait, and in his word do I hope. My soul waiteth for the Lord more than they that watch for the morning; I say more than they that watch for the morning." The Good News Translations states it this way, "I pray to God-my life a prayer-and wait for what he'll say and do. My life's on the line before God, my Lord, waiting and watching till morning, waiting and watching till morning."

The scripture makes reference to those individuals who had the task of watching and keeping guard during the night hours (you know, during that time when your body is programmed to sleep). The indication is that at some point these individuals longed for morning's light so that they could get some relief from their labor (sound familiar?).

The three passages of Scripture presented here provide a framework of sorts as we deal with waiting. I want you to reread them as often as needed, and then ask the Lord to let them speak to your spirit while you wait.

References

Kendrick, S. (2015). The Battle Plan for Prayer: From Basic Training to Targeted Strategies. Nashville, TN: B & H Publishing Group.

King, S. (1999). The Green Mile. New York, NY: Pocket Books.

Maxwell, J. (2002). Maxwell Leadership Bible. Duluth, GA: Maxwell Motivation, Inc.

Peterson, E. (2002). The Message Bible. Colorado Springs, CO: NavPress Publishing Group.

Made in the USA
Columbia, SC
05 June 2025

58858327R10052